For the
Love of Wine

Steamboat Winery's
Year of Wine Facts

by Penney Adams

STEAMBOAT WINERY

SPARK Publications
Charlotte, North Carolina

For the Love of Wine: Steamboat Winery's Year of Wine Facts
Penney Adams

Designed, produced, and published by SPARK Publications
SPARKpublications.com
Charlotte, North Carolina

Photography by Penney Adams

Printed in the United States of America.
Softcover, November 2020, ISBN: 978-1-943070-99-2
Library of Congress Control Number: 2020918026

Dedicated to my dad, Edward L. Daisey, who started me on this wine journey. I am grateful for the memories and love.

Welcome

STEAMBOAT WINERY

Wine is my *joie de vivre*! I adore the places it grows, the history, the growing, the art of winemaking, and of course, the way it tastes, especially with the perfect food pairing. If you have a passion for wine, like me, you will love this book. And if you have an interest in wine, it may just ignite a passion. Steamboat Winery, LLC was established in 2017 in Steamboat Springs, Colorado. Our first vintage was released in the spring of 2019. Our wines have been very well received in our community and nationwide!
In 2019, I started posting a "Wine Fact of the Day" on Instagram. After a few suggestions from customers and friends, I decided to put those facts together in the book you're holding now. I organized the facts into six sections: wine tasting, wine varietals, wine regions, winemaking, wine grapes and growing, and wine history and facts. I chose photographs of our Steamboat Winery life and our wonderful wines to share with you, as well as memorable wine moments I have experienced with friends and family over the years. I hope you will thoroughly enjoy reading the pages of this book, perhaps with a glass or two of one of our fine wines!

Penney Adams

SWI
STEAMBOAT WINERY

RIVER ANGLER

CABERNET

2017

Table of Contents

1

How to taste wine:
1. Swirl and observe the color.
2. Smell and note the aromas.
3. Sip and draw in air over the wine.
4. Move the wine around in your mouth.
5. Swallow and notice the flavors.

2

Wine *tears* or *legs* are a function of the level of alcohol in a wine. The more alcohol, the more wine will stick to the glass after swirling.

3

Smelling a cork reveals little about a wine. Inspect the cork for damage, drying, streaking, mold, or cracking.

4

A 4-ounce glass of wine has 85 calories, but really, who only has 4 ounces?

5

Red wines become lighter in color as they age, while white wines become darker with age.

6 **The five basic characteristics of wine taste are:**
1. Sweetness
2. Acidity
3. Alcohol level
4. Body (or weight)
5. Tannins

7 Opened wine will last for three days if you replace the cork or use a bottle stopper and then place it in the refrigerator. The less contact with the air, the better. Take red wine out an hour before serving.

8 Fill a red wine glass one-third full, a white wine glass half full, and a Champagne flute three-quarters full.

9 When planning how much wine to buy for a party, you should plan on half a bottle of wine per person. However, if you have friends like mine, plan on a bottle!

10 Women generally have a better sense of smell and taste than men.

11 | Does the glass matter? Yes! Each varietal-specific glass has a reason for the shape (for example, the way the wine hits your tongue). At a minimum, you should have a glass big enough for the wine to aerate and for you to smell it.

12 | Approximately 25 percent of the population are supertasters and can have 20,000 taste buds. Taste buds are found all over your mouth, but mostly in the papillae (the pink bumps) on the tongue.

13 | The punt of a bottle is the indentation at the bottom. Many people believe it is there to make the wine easier to pour, but my research indicates it was historically left by glass blowers.

14 | Statistically, women buy more wine than men. United States wine purchases in 2017 were by approximately 59 percent women and 41 percent men.

15 | Tannins, a compound found primarily in red wine, have a bitter, astringent, chalky, or dry taste.

16 | In 2017, millennials (people born between 1981 and 1996) were the largest group of wine buyers in the United States at approximately 40 percent, followed by baby boomers (born between 1946 and 1964).

17 | You should hold a wine glass by the stem, so your hand doesn't change the temperature of the wine, assuming it was served at the proper temperature (or how you like it).

18 | The cheaper the wine, the colder you should serve it. The chill will lessen any "off" aromas and flavors.

19 | Studies have found people fill a glass fuller when pouring white wine versus red.

20 | A wine bottle contains approximately five 5-ounce pours of wine. Five ounces usually hits the glass at the widest point to allow room to smell the aromas (with the exception of a Champagne glass).

21 | It is imperative to take two sips of wine to truly taste it. The flavors change greatly when the salivary juices are flowing and any extraneous residue is rinsed from the mouth.

22 | The amount of wine in your sip determines which flavors you detect. Start with a small cleansing sip followed by a bigger sip.

23 | When decanting an older bottle of wine, use a strainer to capture the sediment or twist the bottle at the end of the pour so that the sediment sticks to the bottle.

24 | Red wines with lower alcohol, high acidity, and tannins age best as they smooth out.

25 | **Some typical white wine pairings:**
Sparkling white · salty food
Dry white · vegetables or salad
Sweet white · spicy food
Rich white · saucy, creamy food

Memorable Wine Moments

When I was five, my mother and my Aunt Joan were lying in the sun in our backyard. With cat-eyed glasses and their hair wrapped in silk scarves, they drank cocktails while I skipped around the yard collecting dandelions for the dandelion wine they would make that afternoon.

26 | **Some typical red wine pairings:**
Light red · simple dishes (cheese, bread, or soup)
Medium red · roasted dishes, Italian cuisine
Bold red · rich meats, stew, or BBQ

27 | *Aroma* is what you smell. *Taste* is what you sense on your tongue. *Flavor* is the combination of aroma and taste.

28 | Wine aromas refer to smells like fruit, herbs, or floral, which comes from the grape varietal. Wine bouquet refers to smells like vanilla, spice, or yeast, which comes from the winemaking process.

29 | The five major tastes are sweet, sour, bitter, salty, and umami.

30 | *Umami* is a savory fullness or richness caused by the interaction of glutamates. It is sometimes found in meat broths or fermented products, like wine.

31 | Wine can be categorized as dry, off-dry, or sweet. *Dry* means unsweet with little residual sugar. *Sweet* refers to the obviously sweet like dessert wine. *Off-dry* is slightly sweet, like a Moscato, with some residual sugar.

32 | *Fruit forward* is a commonly used wine term. It does not mean sweet, but rather the wine has lots of fruit flavors such as blackberry, cherry, apple, lemon, and more.

33 | *Full-bodied* refers to a wine that fills your palate with texture and intensity. Wines with this description often have higher tannins and alcohol levels.

34 | If you are without a corkscrew (an emergency in my opinion), put your bottle of wine in a hard shoe and bang it against a hard surface. The cork should work its way out enough so that you can pull it out.

35 | To chill white wine quickly, wrap it in a wet paper towel and place it in the freezer for fifteen minutes. Just don't forget it or it will likely explode.

36 | If you need to remove a red wine stain, one method is to blot the stain with a paper towel, cover it with salt, and let it sit for one hour. Then dab the stain with hot water.

37 | Another method for removing a red wine stain is to pour white wine on the red wine stain before it sets to remove it. The white wine removes the anthocyanin compounds that give red wine its color.

steamboatwinery.com

38 | To keep your wine cold without watering it down with ice cubes, keep some frozen grapes in the freezer to toss in!

39 | When setting a table with multiple wine glasses, place the water glass above the knife and the wine glasses to the right in the order you will use them from the outside in.

40 | Some different aromas you may find in white wines are citrus (lemon, orange, and grapefruit), stone fruit (peach), tropical fruit (pineapple), apple, and melon.

41 | Some aromas you may find in red wine are red fruit (cherry and strawberry), dark fruit (blackberry and blueberry), stone fruit (plum), or jam (sweeter fruit).

Memorable Wine Moments

On my twenty-first birthday, I shared a bottle of Veuve Clicquot with my parents and a friend at Windows of the World, the restaurant at the top of the World Trade Center's North Tower in New York City. I remember appreciating how fortunate I was to have parents who could provide me with such wonderful experiences. This memory was further etched in my mind after the loss and tragedy of 9/11.

42 | When purchasing a decanter, consider which wine you will be decanting. A fuller bodied wine, like Cabernet Sauvignon, may require more contact with the air found in a wider decanter.

43 | **Some wine and nut pairings:**
Salted almonds · Sparkling wine
Hazelnuts · Chardonnay
Pistachios · Sauvignon Blanc
Spicy nuts · Rosé
Candied nuts · Cabernet Sauvignon
Walnuts · Syrah
Pecans · Barbera

44 | **Some delicious seafood pairings:**
Salmon · Pinot Noir
Oysters · Sparkling wine
Lobster · Chardonnay
Tuna · Rosé
Scallops · Sauvignon Blanc

45 | If you like strawberries, you should try rosé. If you like lemon, you should give Sauvignon Blanc a try. If you like green apples, you might like Chardonnay.

46 Private Preserve is a brand of argon gas in a can. When sprayed into an open bottle, it replaces the oxygen with natural gases that sink in the bottle next to the wine because the gas is heavier than air, which slows down oxidation of the wine, keeping it fresher longer.

47 Wine headaches are most commonly from dehydration and not sulfites. In fact, there are way more sulfites in french fries and dried fruit. Do those give you a headache? Try an antihistamine before drinking the same amount, and if you have no headache, then you may be one of the very few with a wine allergy.

48 Most sediment is removed from wine prior to bottling. Sediment in older red wine comes from the tannins and is a by-product of aging. They are tasteless and harmless, but have a gritty texture.

49 *Tartrates* are crystals sometimes found floating in white wine or attached to the cork. They are tasteless and harmless bits of tartaric acid, also known as cream of tartar.

50 Don't save wine that is going bad for cooking. If it tastes off, it will make your food taste off!

51 | *Wine body* refers to how weighty it feels in your mouth—light (like skim milk), medium, or full bodied (like cream).

52 | The *finish* of a wine refers to how long the taste lingers in your mouth and the textural effect left in your mouth (chalky, smooth, spicy, or bitter).

53 | If you end up with a broken cork in your bottle and do not have a strainer, use a coffee filter to prevent cork pieces from pouring into your glass.

54 | *Minerality* in wine most commonly refers to a taste of flint, wet stone, crushed rock, acidity, or a delicateness indicating wine is not overly fruity or overly oaky.

55 | The *mouthfeel* or texture of a wine is closely related to body, but refers to more than the weight. It can be smooth, gritty, or another texture.

56 | It is recommended that white wines be served at 45–50 degrees and red wines at 50–60 degrees. White wines are often served too cold and red wines too warm.

SWI

STEAMBOAT WINERY

THE DAISIES

SAUVIGNON BLANC

2018

57 | Add frozen fruit to your white wine for added decadence: strawberries for rosé, peaches for Chardonnay, or blueberries for Sauvignon Blanc.

58 | To open sparkling wine, remove the foil cage while keeping your thumb on the cork. With one hand around the cork, twist the bottle to ease the cork out of the bottle and into your hand. Beware—corks can fly at a speed of 55 miles per hour out of a bottle. Several people are killed by corks each year.

59 | Red wine glasses are wider to support oxidation, which is important for red wine. White wines taste best with less oxidation, thus the taller, thinner glass.

Memorable Wine Moments

After being away at college for years, I moved home with my parents. I discovered that while I was away, they would often frequent Carbone's Italian Restaurant in Hartford, Connecticut. They took me there one night. We were greeted with huge smiles and open arms. We sat at "their booth" in the corner and drank a bottle of "their wine." It wasn't anything fancy; I think it was a classic Ruffino Chianti. I definitely remember the straw basket (it's called a fiasco). My mother collected the bottles to take home and melt wax candles all over them to use as centerpieces when we ate her famous spaghetti with meat sauce at home. They loved the connection with the people, the Carbone family, the ambience of the restaurant, the romance of the tradition, and the immense enjoyment of being together, laughing, and loving. They were a perfect example of what true love should look like.

60 Generally speaking, pair your Chardonnay with soft cheeses and your Cabernet Sauvignon with hard cheeses. But don't forget the classic Sauvignon Blanc and goat cheese pairing!

61 One way to determine if a red wine has gone bad is color. Too much oxidation will give it a browner color.

62 **Some wine and chocolate pairings:**
White chocolate covered strawberries · Ranch Dog Rosé
Milk chocolate · Barn Red Blend
Dark chocolate · The Antlers Reserve Cabernet Sauvignon

63 Store wine laying down to keep the cork wet. Storing wines upright can allow the cork to dry out over time and shrink, allowing air to get in and oxidize the wine.

64 Foil cutters cut the foil at the top lip of the bottle. Most servers cut the foil at the bottom lip of the bottle to avoid any interaction when pouring. The foil cap on a bottle of wine is solely for decoration, but conceivably keeps dust off the top of the cork.

65 | When using a waiter's corkscrew, aim the curly metal tip slightly off center to get the corkscrew properly centered for best cork removal.

66 | **If you like this beer, you may like this Steamboat Winery wine:**
Wheat · Slopeside White Chardonnay
Pilsner · The Daisies Sauvignon Blanc
Lager · Barn Red Blend
Amber · The Antlers Reserve Cabernet Sauvignon

67 | Too little humidity can cause a cork to dry out and allow air to oxidize the wine. Too much humidity can cause mold and loosen labels. The ideal humidity for wine storage is 70 percent.

68 | *Velvety* is a word often used to describe a smooth-tasting red wine with soft tannins.

69 | It is best to let red wines *breathe* in a decanter (even young red wines). It is not enough to just pop the cork; the only wine getting aerated in that case is the wine in the neck of the bottle.

70 | A wine that is referred to as *tight* is not as flavorful as it could be, usually because it is young.

71 | Younger red wines are healthier than older red wines because they have more tannins.

72 | You should store your crystal wine glasses upright. The upper rim is the most fragile part of the glass.

Memorable Wine Moments

I came home after a summer during college, and my mother suggested we go out for a nice dinner. I put on a dress I bought for myself with my summer earnings. She brought me to The Bee and Thistle Inn in Chester, Connecticut. She ordered us a bottle of Grgich Hills Chardonnay, which we enjoyed with a lovely dinner. It was a turning point in our relationship. We now related more as individuals, great friends, rather than being under her direction and guidance as mother/daughter. I had become an independent young lady, although she remained there for guidance when I needed and asked for it for the rest of our time together.

73 | The best way to clean your decanter is to soak it in warm water, rinse it out with a tablespoon of white wine vinegar mixed with water, and then rinse it with warm water. Do not put in the dishwasher!

74 | Many red wines are worth aging, but few white varietals are. Two whites known for ageability are white Burgundy and Riesling.

75 | According to wine expert, Robert Parker, the best recent vintages for northern California Cabernet Sauvignon are 2016, 2015, and 2013.

Memorable Wine Moments

My parents had a house on a lake in Vermont where we would visit every Fourth of July. We would take the whole family (my parents, sisters, and our children) out on the boat to sip wine, often Pouilly Fuissé, watch the fireworks, and listen to the sound echo off the surrounding mountains. We were very close and shared many of these spectacular moments.

Wine Varietals

76 | It can only be called "Champagne" if it's from the Champagne region of France. Everywhere else, it is called sparkling wine. Either way, cheers!

77 | Blanc de noir designates a Champagne made with Pinot Noir or Pinot Meunier, while a blanc de blanc is a Champagne made with only Chardonnay grapes.

78 | Pouilly-Fuissé is a crisp, clean (not overly buttery) Chardonnay from Mâconnais in Burgundy.

79 | Gamay is the varietal used to make the French wine Beaujolais. It is a light red wine with very low tannins.

80 | Beaujolais is made in three categories: Beaujolais, Beaujolais Villages, and Beaujolais cru.

81 | Bordeaux wine in France is ranked into *growths*, with the best being *first growths*. Grand cru and *premiere cru* generally translate to *great growth* and *first growth*, respectively. The terms denote a level of quality but are not used consistently in every region.

82 | A red Bordeaux is primarily made up of Cabernet Sauvignon, Merlot, and Cabernet Franc. A white Bordeaux is primarily made up of Sauvignon Blanc and Semillon.

83 | Cinsault, also called cinsaut, is a red grape used often for blending in French Rhône wines.

84 | Sauternes is a French sweet dessert wine from the Sauternais region of France. Château d'Yquem is one of the most famous French dessert wines.

85 | Red Burgundy from France is made with the Pinot Noir grape, and white Burgundy is made with the Chardonnay grape.

Memorable Wine Moments

While living in Charlotte, North Carolina, my parents came to visit me for Thanksgiving. My mother bought me an antique wine rack made from wood removed from an old shoe factory and then insisted we go to a wine store so that she could fill it. With the turkey in the oven, we chose a white Burgundy from Leflaive from the rack, and we all sat at the kitchen table with charcuterie. We drank, ate, and talked, thoroughly enjoying our conversation. We opened more wine. We continued to eat, talk, and laugh. I felt immensely grateful to have parents whose company I so enjoyed. We were having such a fun time that we decided not to cook the rest of the Thanksgiving meal. We stayed at the table connecting and had Thanksgiving dinner the next day. She was gone shortly after; I am so fond of that happy memory.

86 | Puligny-Montrachet is a Chardonnay from Burgundy, well known as a silky, elegant, and very fine wine.

87 | White Rhône blends from France are typically made from Roussanne, Marsanne, and Viognier.

88 | If you like light, dry white wine, you might try a Chablis—a Chardonnay from France, typically unoaked.

89 | Two popular wines from the Piedmont region of Italy are Barolo and Barbaresco, both made from the Nebbiolo grape.

90 | Sangiovese is widely grown in the Tuscany region of Italy. It is used to make Chianti, Brunello di Montalcino, and Super Tuscans. (Some are blended with other grapes as well.)

91 | Barbera is a poplar grape in Italy known for its deep purple grape color, ruby-red wine color, bold flavor, and light tannins.

92 | Barbera has berry flavors, high acidity, and subtle tannins compared to varietals like Cabernet Sauvignon that are more tannic.

93 | Some call Barbera "Italy's Pinot Noir." It's light, delicious, and like many Italian wines, is best accompanying food (ribs, beef roast, saucy chicken, and veal).

94 | Soave is an Italian white from Veneto made with Gargenega. It is crisp, light, and similar in style to Pinot Grigio.

95 | Prosecco, Italian sparkling wine, differs from Champagne in that the second fermentation is done in a tank rather than the bottle, which often makes it lighter, fruitier, and more floral.

Memorable Wine Moments

I once accompanied my father to a wine dinner at the home of a man with a passion for wine. He had stations of wine paired with gourmet food around his home, which concluded in his wine cellar, where we drank an aged Warre's Vintage Port paired with chocolate truffles. The spark of curiosity for wine knowledge ignited in me.

96 | For a Chianti to carry the Italian DOC certification (a quality certification similar to the French AOC), it needs to be made with at least 80 percent Sangiovese and made in the Chianti region of Italy.

97 | Moscato is made with the Muscat grape mostly in northern Italy. It is often consumed as a dessert wine. Paired with a strong bleu cheese—amazing!

98 | Pinot Gris made in Oregon is the same grape used in Italy's Pinot Grigio.

99 | Three of the most well-known Super Tuscans are Sassicaia, Ornellaia, and Tignanello. Highly sought-after vintages of Sassicaia can cost up to $4,000!

100 | Rosé is growing in popularity. Exports from Provence have increased tremendously, and many California vineyards are producing delicious rosé (not to be confused with sweet White Zinfandel).

101 | While Cabernet Sauvignon and Sauvignon Blanc generally prefer warmer climates, Pinot Noir and Riesling generally prefer cooler climates. Chardonnay is a varietal that grows well in both!

102 | Chardonnay is the most widely planted white varietal in the world and the most popular wine in the United States.

103 | Alcohol levels of Chardonnay typically range from 12 to 15 percent, with lighter, fruitier Chardonnay being lower, and rich, flavorful Chardonnay being higher.

104 | **Some white wines listed from dry to sweet:** Sauvignon Blanc, Pinot Grigio, Chardonnay, Viognier, Gewürztraminer, Riesling, and Moscato.

105 | **Some red wines listed from dry to sweet:** Sangiovese, Cabernet Sauvignon, Pinot Noir, Syrah, Merlot, Zinfandel, and port.

106 | Seventy-five percent of the wines from Alsace are made with single varietals (100 percent of one grape variety) of Riesling, Pinot Blanc, Gewürztraminer, or Pinot Gris.

Memorable Wine Moments

My entire family went on a skiing vacation in Austria. On our last evening, we shared a private dinner in the rustic wine cellar of the resort. We had several delicious bottles, but I particularly remember one, Angelus Bordeaux, because I recall thinking our angel, my mother, Jane, was with us.

107 | If you are looking for a German Riesling that is not sweet, look for the word *trocken* (dry) on the label. Generally, next in sweetness would be *kabinett*, *spatlese*, and the very sweet would be labeled *auslese*.

108 | Rosé made from Pinot Noir or Grenache tends to be more pink than rosé made from Syrah or Sangiovese, which can be more orange in color and have more of a spice in the taste.

109 | Rosé is unique in that it is best enjoyed immediately and definitely within two years of pressing.

110 | The color of a wine is a strong clue to the varietal. Pinot Noir is generally a pale ruby color, while Cabernet Sauvignon is deep ruby, Zinfandel is deep red, and Syrah generally has a purple hue.

111 | If you like Sauvignon Blanc, an Austrian Grüner Veltliner is a similar style of wine with acidic, lime, lemon, and grapefruit flavors. Try one!

112 | If you are a California Chardonnay fan, you may like another full-bodied white varietal such as Viognier.

SWI
STEAMBOAT WINERY

BARN RED

RED WINE BLEND

2018

113	Viognier is lush and aromatic with notes of pear, peach, violet, and sometimes a faint minerality. Originally a Rhône varietal, it is now found in many different countries, including the USA.
114	Chardonnay can be very diverse—from crisp and minerally to buttery and creamy—depending on where it's grown and the winemaking style. It is often oaked, which can add toasty, vanilla flavors.
115	Syrah has a dark, rich color, is very aromatic, and higher in tannins.
116	Syrah is known for its great pairing with venison and lamb. We love our Expert Slope Syrah with barbecue.

Memorable Wine Moments

My father and I started buying wine futures of French Bordeaux and Napa Cabernet Sauvignon. I started a vertical collection of Mouton Rothschild, beginning with my son Edward's birth year of 1992. We traveled to Washington, DC, for future tastings at the French embassy, where we heard presentations from wine experts like Robert Parker and enjoyed some fabulous wine together. It was then I decided I wanted to be in the wine business.

117 | A popular Rhône varietal, Syrah originated in France. It is the same grape known as Shiraz in Australia.

118 | Syrah is often blended with Viognier (yes, a white wine) for its aroma.

119 | Shiraz from Australia, verses Syrah from France or California, is more jammy and not generally as good for aging.

120 | Shiraz is the most widely planted grape in Australia.

121 | Grenache is one of the most widely planted grapes in the world. It grows best in hot, dry areas like Spain.

122 | Châteauneuf-du-Pape is a pricey Rhône wine made primarily with Grenache.

123 | Rioja is a Spanish red wine from the Rioja region of Spain, made primarily with the Tempranillo grape. It pairs well with strong cheeses and meats.

124 | **Rioja has four classifications:** Rioja, Crianza, Reserva, and Gran Reserva. Gran Reserva is made with the best grapes and aged the longest.

125 | Syrah and Petit Sirah are two different grapes entirely. Ironically, Petite Sirah is not little or lighter, but usually much bolder, darker in color, and heavier in texture.

126 | Carignan is a red wine varietal that originated in Spain, marked by high acidity and tannins.

127 | Pinotage is a South-African varietal. It is a cross between a Pinot Noir and a Cinsault.

128 | Chenin Blanc is known as a Pineau de la Loire, a crisp acidic white grape from Loire, France. In South Africa, some refer to it as Steen.

For the *Love of Wine*

129 | Colombard wine is a white varietal that originated in France. It is an offspring of Chenin Blanc and is now grown widely in South Africa.

130 | Some wines that are typically higher in alcohol are Grenache, Pinotage, Zinfandel, and Petite Sirah.

131 | Port, mainly from Portugal, is a fortified, sweet dessert wine. It is generally either ruby or tawny. Some wonderful aged ports pair nicely with chocolate or blue cheese.

132 | Vinho Verde, from Portugal, is a slightly effervescent, usually white (but sometimes red), crisp, acidic, and refreshing wine.

Memorable Wine Moments

I took a wine cruise along the Russian River after running the Marine Corp Marathon. We stopped at Matanzas Creek Winery and enjoyed a private dinner. I remember walking through their lavender fields with a glass of wine, in awe of the surrounding beauty and taste of the great wine.

133 | Merlot is typically less expensive than Cabernet Sauvignon, particularly in the United States. Merlot is fruit driven, less tannic, has a smooth finish, and is sometimes perceived as less complex.

134 | Malbec originated in France as a Bordeaux blending grape but is now quite popular on its own. It is widely planted in Argentina and known for its big, bold flavor.

135 | If you are looking for wines with fewer carbs, choose dry varietals like Sauvignon Blanc and rosé.

Wine Regions

136 In 1976, there was an infamous Paris blind tasting where two California wines—Chateau Montelena Chardonnay and Stag's Leap Wine Cellars Cabernet Sauvignon—won the competition against several well-known French wines. They helped to put California wines on the map and remain excellent wines to this day!

137 France produces the most wine annually, followed by Italy, Spain, and the United States.

138 For a wine to be called "Cabernet Sauvignon" or any other grape varietal in the United States, it is required the wine be made with 75 percent of the named grape varietal. The requirement is 85 percent in France, Italy, Germany, and several other countries.

139 Wines from France are named after the region they are from, such as Burgundy and Bordeaux. Wines from the United States are named after the grape variety used to make them, such as Cabernet Sauvignon, and and Chardonnay.

140 | Two well-known areas of the Loire Valley in France are Sancerre and Pouilly-Fumé, wine regions known for Sauvignon Blanc. The Touraine, Samur, Chinon, and Vouvray wine regions are dominated by Chenin Blanc and Cabernet Franc.

141 | **The 1855 Bordeaux Classification distinguished the four first growths:** Châteaux Margaux, Lafite-Rothschild, Châteaux Latour, and Haut-Brion. Mouton Rothschild was added later.

142 | Approximately 90 percent of all wine produced in Provence is rosé.

143 | Provence is the oldest wine region in France, and rosé is the oldest known wine. Dubbed the "wine of freedom," rosé has shown rapid growth in popularity, particularly among millennials, and appears to be here to stay!

Memorable Wine Moments

One evening at my wine store, The Wine Gallery, the power went out. A small group of friends remained. Our guitarist played on acoustically while we enjoyed some candlelit Darioush Cabernet Sauvignon, meaningful conversation, and friendship.

144 | The French call wines to save *vins de garde*. Not all wines age well; most rosé and white wines are meant to be consumed young.

145 | In France, much more red wine is consumed than white wine. More rosé is consumed than white wine as well.

146 | More white Burgundy is made than red Burgundy in France.

147 | The major regions of Burgundy are Chablis, Côte de Nuits, Côte de Beaune, Côte Chalonnaise, and Mâconnais.

148 | The name *Bordeaux* comes from *au bord de l'eau* which means "along the waters."

149 | The major regions of Bordeaux for red Bordeaux wines are Margaux, Pauillac, Pomerol, Graves, Saint-Émilion, Saint-Estèphe, and Saint-Julien.

150 | More than 60 percent of the vines planted in Bordeaux are Merlot.

151 | Beaujolais Nouveau is released the third Thursday in November. Producers roll barrels through torchlit streets in the Beaujolais region of France.

152 | Beaujolais Nouveau is a wine rich in tradition; it is historically released just weeks after fermentation as a marketing ploy invented to help with cashflow.

153 | Alsace in France sits between the Rhine River and the Vosges mountains, which protect the region from rainfall and create a warm, dry summer with a slope perfect for growing grapes, especially Riesling.

154 | Côtes du Rhône is a wine region in France whose wine is made primarily from Syrah and Grenache.

155 | Left Bank wines of Bordeaux are typically dominated by Cabernet Sauvignon, while Right Bank wines are dominated by Merlot.

156 Over 90 percent of wine production in the United States is in California, Washington, and Oregon.

157 The five states that drink the most wine in America in 2018 are California, Florida, New York, Texas, and Illinois. Wine drinking per capita shows a different picture: Idaho, Delaware, New Hampshire, New Mexico, and Vermont.

158 Malbec is probably the most famous wine made in Argentina, but they produce many other varietals, including Cabernet, Merlot, Syrah, Chardonnay, Bonarda, and Torrontes.

159 Chardonnay and Pinot Noir are made in New Zealand, but the country is most widely known for its Sauvignon Blanc.

Memorable Wine Moments

My Italian friend and wine importer hosted a wine dinner for me and some of my best girlfriends at my wine store. We played Italian music and savored authentic Italian food by candlelight with several great Italian wines. He told fantastic stories in his intoxicating accent.

160 | South Africa is known for its Pinotage (a cross between Pinot Noir and Cinsault), as well as its Syrah and Cabernet Sauvignon.

161 | *Claret* is a British term for red Bordeaux, which is typically a blend of Cabernet Sauvignon, Merlot, and Cabernet Franc.

162 | It's called *rosé* in France, *rosato* in Italy, and *rosado* in Spain, not to be confused with *blush*, a semisweet wine.

163 | The Chianti district is known as the "Heart of Tuscany."

164 | Dolcetto is grown in the Piedmont region of Italy; it is known for black cherry, licorice, and prune flavors.

165 | Vermentino is a white grape varietal widely planted in Sardinia, Italy. It is similar to Sauvignon Blanc—citrusy, light, crisp, and generally unoaked.

166 | Merlot originated in France as both a blending grape and an independent varietal. The grapes on the vine are dark blue, almost black. The name Merlot was derived from the French word *merle*, which means blackbird.

167 | Sonoma's Russian River Valley is known for its cool climate and fog due to the Pacific Ocean influence. It is an ideal place to grow Chardonnay and Pinot Noir. It happens to be where our 2017 Slopeside White Chardonnay grapes are from!

168 | Michigan was one of the first states to make wine in the 1670s. Bunny Slope, our nonalcoholic sparkling grape juice, is made with grapes from Paw Paw, Michigan.

169 | While there are some southern regions in Napa known for Pinot Noir and some northern regions known for Zinfandel, Napa Valley is world renowned for Chardonnay and Cabernet Sauvignon.

170 | Approximately 95 percent of all Napa Valley wineries are family owned.

171 | Old World wines are from Europe. New World wines are from everywhere else. Our California and Colorado wines are New World.

172 | The Lodi region is located in the northern part of California's Central Valley. It is known for its old vine Zinfandels and happens to be where our Expert Slope Syrah and The Aspens Barbera grapes are from.

173 | Within Sonoma County are seventeen designated AVAs (American Viticulture Areas). It is the most diverse premium-grape growing region in the US, with valleys, hills, mountains, and a coastline.

174 | There are over 400 wineries in Napa, which produce over 800 different wine brands.

175 | Napa means "land of plenty" in the language of the Wappo indigenous people. The thirteen AVAs (American Viticulture Areas) in Napa benefit from its Mediterranean climate.

176 | While Chardonnay is the most widely sold wine varietal in the United States, Cabernet Sauvignon is the most widely sold wine varietal in the world.

177 | California grows more Chardonnay than any place else in the world.

178 | While Napa is much smaller than Sonoma, many more wineries are in Napa.

179 | Why Napa Cabernet Sauvignon? The region boasts warm days for grapes to ripen and create sugars, cool nights for vines to rest and keep acid levels up, and rain only between November and February, which creates a long growing season. Just try our River Angler Cabernet Sauvignon or The Antlers Reserve Cabernet Sauvignon, and you will understand.

180 | Many stories surround the original meaning of the word *sonoma*. Two of them are "valley of the moon" and "abandoned camping place."

181	Sixty-six percent of wine purchased in the United States in 2019 was produced in the United States while 34 percent was imported.
182	*Paso Robles* is technically pronounced *roh-buhlz*, although in Spanish it is pronounced *roh-blays*.
183	Amador County is in the Sierra Foothills where Zinfandel is most widely planted. However, now you can find great Syrah, Barbera, and Sangiovese from there as well.
184	Seated between two mountain ranges, Santa Barbera, California, has a cool climate that grows wonderful Pinot Noir and Chardonnay.

Memorable Wine Moments

I once traveled to Napa with three close girlfriends. We went to many fabulous places, but I particularly remember sipping delicious Phelps Insignia on the porch of Joseph Phelps, sharing intimate details of our lives and connecting.

185 | Four popular wine regions of Chile are Coquimbo, Aconcagua, Central Valley, and South Region. You can find Chardonnay, Syrah, and Cabernet Sauvignon in all of those regions.

186 | Wine is produced in all fifty states, but almost 90 percent of the total production is in California.

187 | The Moon Mountain District AVA is located in Sonoma and known for old vine Zinfandel and Cabernet Sauvignon.

188 | Chilean wine is growing in popularity. Cabernet Sauvignon, Merlot, and Carménère make up about 75 percent of its production.

189 | Dom Perignon was a monk and winemaker. He discovered many different winemaking techniques, including capturing bubbles in wine.

190 | Willamette is one of the sixteen growing regions in Oregon. The easiest way to remember how to pronounce it? Willamette rhymes with damn it!

191 | Fourteen wine regions are in Washington state, focusing primarily on Cabernet Sauvignon, Merlot, Syrah, Chardonnay, and Riesling, covering more than 55,000 acres.

192 | Four countries that produce delicious wine at a great value are Spain, Italy, Chile, and Australia, based on ratings and price.

193 | *Appellation* is a legally defined area where the grapes for a particular wine are grown.

Memorable Wine Moments

On my father's seventieth birthday, my family gathered in a small German village and had a wonderful alfresco dinner at the Vogelbauer Restaurant. It was a bucolic old barn and evening. A harpist serenaded our table in the setting sun. Chickens ran by as we enjoyed a bottle of Gaja Rossj-Bass Chardonnay and a Sassicaia Super Tuscan with an incredible meal.

Winemaking

194 | Tannins are derived from grape skins, seeds, and stems, or from the oak barrel that was used to age the wine.

195 | In the fall, many vines are covered in netting to keep the birds from eating the tasty, sweet grapes.

196 | White wine can be made with red grapes if the juice is pressed and the wine does not come in contact with the skins.

197 | Sparkling wine is typically made with a second fermentation where yeast and sugar are added to the wine. This creates carbon dioxide bubbles, which get trapped in the wine.

198 | Only about 10 percent of wineries are owned by women. Steamboat Winery is proud to be one!

199 | There are approximately sixty gallons of wine in a barrel, or about twenty-five cases of wine (300 bottles).

For the *Love of Wine*

200 | *Brut* is a term used to indicate a Champagne or sparkling wine that is very dry and not sweet. In fact, brut is drier than extra dry Champagne or sparkling wine.

201 | The United States has no regulation on using the word *reserve* on a label. However, winemakers typically do save this title for their best wines.

202 | Unfiltered wines are increasing in popularity. Some winemakers believe filtering removes much of the flavor and character of the wine and prefer the more natural process. Our 2017 Slopeside White Chardonnay is unfiltered.

203 | Sulfites occur naturally in wine and can also be added by the winemaker to preserve wine.

Memorable Wine Moments

My sisters and I traveled to Paris together. After visiting the Louvre Museum, we shared a bottle of Perrier Jouet Champagne at an outdoor café and ate the most delicious fresh bread and soft cheese while reminiscing about our mother.

204 Despite some recent popular opinions, sulfites are not all bad. A small amount of added sulfites prevents bacteria from growing and helps to preserve the wine.

205 Generally, red wine has fewer sulfites than white wines do because red wines are more chemically stable and preserve better.

206 *Brix* is a measure of sugar in wine grapes that ultimately determines the amount of alcohol in a wine.

207 Picking grapes too early can lead to more acid and less alcohol. The trick is to harvest the grapes at optimal acid and alcohol levels, which is later, but sometimes the weather dictates earlier picking than desired.

208 Alcohol levels in wine can be deceiving. The level is listed on the label as percent ABV, meaning alcohol by volume. Legally the label can be 1.5 percent off for wines under 14 percent ABV and 1 percent off for wines over 14 percent ABV. The typical range of alcohol levels in wine is 10-15 percent.

209 | It takes approximately one cluster, or seventy-five grapes, to make a glass of wine.

210 | *Enology* is the study of wines and winemaking. *Viticulture* is the cultivation and harvesting of grapes.

211 | Red blends are increasing in popularity, surpassing rosé and sparkling wine sales in the US! Have you tried our Barn Red Blend of Merlot and Cabernet Sauvignon?

212 | *Chaptalization* is the process of adding sugar to grapes to create more sugar for yeast to ferment into alcohol. It is only legal in some areas that grow grapes low in sugar.

213 | *Brettanomyces* is a naturally occurring yeast often associated with wine spoilage. "Brett" causes a barnyard smell in wine when there is too much growth.

214 | *Malolactic fermentation* is a process in winemaking. It is most recognizable in Chardonnay, resulting in a buttery flavor. During fermentation, naturally occurring acid is converted to a smoother tasting acid. This can happen naturally or be manipulated by a winemaker.

215 | *Must* is freshly crushed grape juice that contains the skin, seeds, and stems. The solid portion of the must is called *pomace*.

216 | *Bottle shock*, besides a fabulous movie, occurs when wine is first bottled or makes a long journey. It can taste flat or dull due to the compounds jostling. It will return to its great flavor after resting.

217 | *Maceration* is the process in winemaking of leaving the grape skins in contact with the juice until it reaches the desired color and tannin. With rosé, the red skins are left in contact with the juice for just a few days to give it very little color.

Memorable Wine Moments

I was newly divorced and had a speaking event in Palm Springs. After, I took my first vacation alone and drove up the coast of California. On my way to the JUST Inn in Paso Robles, home of Justin Vineyards, I drove through the winding roads with the bright sun low in the sky. I was greeted by their two labrador retrievers in the driveway and checked into my room. As I sat on the porch, with a glass of Isosceles and charcuterie, a full moon appeared behind the vine-covered mountains. Although I was alone, I felt incredibly happy.

218 | Louis Pasteur determined the exact process of alcohol fermentation in the mid-1800s.

219 | The *lees* in winemaking are the leftover, dead yeast cells and residual particles that separate from the wine during fermentation and are typically removed. Some wine is aged "on the lees," which some feel gives it more body and complex flavor. Our 2017 Slopeside White Chardonnay was aged on the lees.

220 | *Racking* wine means separating the wine from the lees through a filtering process.

221 | *Punching down the wine* is a phrase used to describe pressing down the grape skins during fermentation.

222 | You may see *spumante* or *frizzante* on your Italian wine label. Spumante means sparkling wine, while frizzante means gently sparkling.

223 | There are generally two types of wine barrels—French oak and American oak.

224 | Wine barrels are toasted on the inside during production to help bring out flavors in the oak, such as vanilla, crème brûlée, and spice, thus adding these flavors to the wine aged in the barrel.

225 | Most wines are barrel-aged for less than a year, but others are aged for years. Some of our red wines are aged for over two years.

226 | Aged in "neutral oak" means a wine that was aged in a barrel that is over three years old and no longer impacts the flavor of the wine but can soften it.

227 | Primary fermentation of wine usually lasts three to seven days. Seventy percent of the alcohol is created during this process.

Memorable Wine Moments

I have watched the Oscars with the same group of twelve ladies for over twenty-five years. Each year, we drink Veuve Clicquot Champagne and celebrate each other and our incredible and unremitting friendship.

228 | Secondary fermentation in winemaking usually lasts one to two weeks. The air is removed, signaling the yeast to stop multiplying and convert the remaining sugar into alcohol.

229 | *Riddling* is the daily slight rotation of an inverted Champagne bottle in a riddler (rack) to get the sediment in the neck of the bottle for release. Manual riddling can take four to six weeks.

230 | Wine is a living process and changes in the bottle, which is why proper wine storage is so important.

231 | A *wine thief* is a tool used to extract a small amount of wine from the barrel.

232 | American oak barrels give wines more intense flavor than French oak barrels. It imparts more flavors of vanilla, sweet spice, or coconut. French oak barrels impart more a subtle flavor and firmer yet silkier tannins.

233 The newer a barrel, the more flavor it imparts to the wine. The smaller the barrel, the more influenced the wine is with oak flavors.

234 You typically save money buying wine directly from a winery because you are avoiding the expense of a wholesaler, distributor, and retailer.

235 Wine that evaporates from a wine barrel is referred to as the *angel's share*. It is important to keep a wine barrel completely full to avoid contact with air.

236 Sparkling wine is difficult to make because it requires two fermentations—one to make the wine and one to make the bubbles.

237 **There are two popular methods of making sparkling wine:** traditional (second fermentation done inside the bottle) and tank (second fermentation done in a tank and then bottled).

238 | A glass of Champagne has approximately fifty-six million bubbles.

239 | *Tirage* is the process of adding yeast and sugar to wine to create a second fermentation to make a sparkling wine.

240 | *Disgorging* is the removal of sediment (or lees) in the neck of a bottle after the second fermentation of a sparkling wine.

241 | *Dosage* is the wine and sugar added to sparkling wine, after disgorgement, to fill the bottle.

242 | Burgundy barrels are shorter and fatter than Bordeaux barrels. They are better suited for making Chardonnay and hold a little more wine.

243 | *Methoxypyrazine* (or just pyrazine) is a grassy, herbaceous-aroma compound often associated with Sauvignon Blanc and Cabernet Sauvignon. Some say it smells like bell pepper, but it smells like grass to me.

244 | On average, an acre of land produces five tons of grapes or 300 cases of wine. Yields can vary from two to ten tons per acre depending on area, year, and so forth.

245 | Things that are worth paying more for in wine are premium grapes, hand-picked grapes, and barrel-aged wine.

246 | A stable wine is one in which all fermentation has stopped for good. A wine must be stable prior to bottling.

247 | Mouthwash contains more alcohol than wine does.

Memorable Wine Moments

When first dating, my husband and I visited my father in Nantucket on the weekend of the Nantucket Wine Festival. It began with a Duckhorn wine dinner at my very favorite restaurant, The Summer House. I fell in love among the rose-covered cottages, secret paths, ocean air, and spectacular wine. We later served Duckhorn wines at our wedding.

248 Generally, for wine to be certified kosher, it must be made under the supervision of a rabbi using only kosher ingredients and must only be handled from growing to finished wine by Sabbath-observant Jewish people.

249 Winemakers can control how fast and intense a fermentation is, which can greatly affect the flavor of the wine. The cooler the fermentation, the slower the yeast ferments. Slower fermentation can produce more complex and more aromatic wine. Our Ranch Dog Rosé was made in this fashion.

250 **There are four basic techniques for making rosé:** limited maceration, bleeding (saignée), pressing, and runoff.

251 Statistics show people will pay more money for wine in a heavier bottle and if the wine name is hard to pronounce. Our Antlers Reserve Cabernet Sauvignon is bottled in a heavy, beautiful bottle, but we only charge more for the premium Napa grapes!

RANCH DOG
ROSÉ WINE
2019

THE DAISIES
SAUVIGNON BLANC
2019

RIVER ANGLER
CABERNET
2017

THE ANTLERS
RESERVE
CABERNET SAUVIGNON
2017

252 | Home winemaking was illegal until 1979.

253 | All grape juice starts out clear.

254 | Three things that help preserve wine in the bottle are sugar, acid, and tannins.

255 | Oak wood chips can be added to age a wine instead of putting it in an oak barrel.

256 | A "corked" wine is one that has been tainted with TCA (2,4,6-trichloroanisole), which is formed when natural fungi in the cork comes in contact with certain winery sanitation chlorides. The wine could smell or taste a little off, or have a strong, foul, musty smell.

257 | Due to TCA that causes "corked" wine, corks are no longer washed in chlorine, but wineries still wash barrels and equipment with water that contains chlorine, which could cause cork tainting.

258 | Fortified wine is wine with brandy or another spirit added to it.

259 | Some large cork manufacturers have said they are capable of completely eliminating cork taint. We may see a cork reemergence one day.

260 | *Cuvee* is a French word meaning vat or tank, but when used with wine, it typically denotes a high-quality blend of grapes.

261 | A bottle of wine is approximately 86 percent water.

262

Some standard bottle sizes are:
Magnum = 2 bottles
Double Magnum = 4 bottles
Jeroboam = 6 bottles
Methuselah or Imperial = 8 bottles
Salmanazar = 12 bottles
Balthazar = 16 bottles
Nebuchadnezzar = 20 bottles

263

A Champagne or sparkling wine bottle is typically thicker than a regular wine bottle to withstand the pressure of carbonation.

264

Record high temperatures has Champagne considering new varietals and new methods of winemaking. Grapes have been ripening too fast, creating lower acid levels.

Wine Grapes
and Growing

265 | *Terroir* is a French word that describes characteristics of land in which grapes are grown, such as soil and climate, that give it a unique taste specific to that land or vineyard.

266 | Newly planted vines take three to five years to produce grapes that can be harvested. It takes passion and commitment to make an investment like that!

267 | There are over 10,000 varieties of wine grapes in the world.

268 | *Vitis vinifera* is the common grapevine that is the main source of Old World wine, such as Chardonnay, Cabernet Sauvignon, and Pinot Noir.

269 | *Viticulture* is the growing of grapevines. *Viniculture* is the cultivation of grapevines specifically for winemaking.

270 | Table grapes that you buy in the grocery store have thinner skins and more seeds than grapes used to make wine.

271 | Niagra grapes are the leading table grapes grown in the United States. Our Bunny Slope nonalcoholic sparkling grape juice, created by my boys, Jeff and Alston, is 100 percent Niagra grapes.

272 | The word *château* typically refers to a French vineyard estate.

273 | Newly planted vines are placed in growing tubes to keep the baby vines protected from wind, pests, and disease.

Memorable Wine Moments

One crisp fall day, my husband took my best friend, Michele Melville, and me by boat from Hilton Head to Buffalo's, a favorite restaurant in Palmetto Bluff. We sat bundled outside in the sun, ate lunch, and drank a bottle of Cakebread Sauvignon Blanc while discussing the beauties and meaning of life.

274 Grapes grown in warmer climates are riper when picked and typically sweeter, which tends to produce bolder fruit flavors and more alcohol. Grapes grown in cooler climates are generally more tart and produce subtle fruit flavors and less alcohol.

275 The average growing season for grapes is 180 days. Our growing season here in the mountains of Steamboat Springs, Colorado, is usually less than 100 days, not long enough for consistent wine grape growing.

276 At first bud break on the vines in spring, winemakers watch carefully for freezing temperatures at night that could harm new shoots. Large fans or sprinklers are sometimes used to protect them.

277 Grapes with a longer ripening time (hang time) produce wines with more developed and complex flavors.

278 *Thinning the fruit* is a phrase used to describe pruning the flower blooms (that become grapes) to focus the energy on the remaining leaves, vines, and roots in order to produce a greater yield the following year.

279 | An ideal summer for grapes has mild days and cool nights with no rain and no heat wave.

280 | Fog is often a moderating factor in grape growing, acting as a cooling agent in warmer climates.

281 | The canopy of grape vines refers to everything visible about ground: vines, leaves, shoots, trunk, fruit, and flowers.

282 | The vine canopy is important for capturing light and energy to begin the process of photosynthesis.

283 | Canopy management or pruning is a delicate balance; too much will cause small crops, too little will cause over-cropping and low-quality fruit. It is a skill that requires experience and good judgment.

284 | White grapes are typically harvested earlier than red grapes. Champagne grapes are usually the first harvested.

285 | Vines prefer a cool, wet winter providing plenty of groundwater and a spring without much rain. A lack of rain is also important preceding and during harvest.

286 | Ideal wine often comes from vines minimally irrigated and moderately stressed.

287 | The vintage year on a wine bottle is always the year the grapes were harvested, rather than the year the wine was bottled after barrel aging.

Memorable Wine Moments

One spring evening, my group of twelve girlfriends got together to watch the Charlotte Symphony Orchestra play an outdoor concert. Someone brought the "Friendship Ball," a gift we have passed around for over twenty years with a notebook that details the date and reason given. We delighted in Groth Sauvignon Blanc wine while someone read the book to us all with a flashlight. It took us on a journey back through the celebrations and difficult times in our lives and reminded us of our profound love and friendship.

288 | Wine labeled *old vine* is not regulated, although it is generally understood to be vines over twenty years old when they are less productive but highly concentrated and intense, producing a wine that some perceive as better.

289 | *Whole cluster fermentation* is fermenting the grapes with the stems (or some percentage of stems). Some winemakers believe this achieves greater complexity and better tannins.

290 | The term *organic* in the United States means a wine organically grown (without pesticides) and without added sulfites. There may be other additives. In Europe, organic wines may include added sulfites.

291 | *Biodynamics* is a holistic view of agriculture. A biodynamic wine is made according to the biodynamic calendar and takes organic farming to the next level, incorporating the connectivity of the vine, moon, planet, and stars.

SWI

STEAMBOAT WINERY

NNY SLOPE

— ALCOHOLIC —

RED GRAPE JUICE

50 ML

292 | The grapes used to make Champagne are primarily Chardonnay, Pinot Noir, and Pinot Meunier.

293 | Eiswein, or ice wine, was invented in Germany. The grapes are frozen on the vine and picked right away, creating a highly concentrated and sweet dessert wine.

294 | The optimal viticulture scenario for vine growth is a continuously cold winter (but not Steamboat cold) followed by a continuously warm spring and summer.

295 | Flowering occurs in spring, which is when grape clusters pollinate themselves. Every fertilized flower becomes a grape.

296 | Soil plays a very important role in the character of a wine. Soil can retain heat, reflect sunlight, and affect water drainage. Vines can grow in over thirty very different soil types.

297 | Vine spacing is important. The closer vines are spaced together, the more the vines compete for the same soil, nutrients, and water, which can increase quality. Experts are constantly searching for the proper balance.

298 | Vines that grow on a hillside, exposed to sun and wind, tend to produce grapes with thicker skins and therefore higher, bolder tannins. Could this be where the phrase "thick-skinned" came from? Exposed and stressed, making them tough?

299 | The health benefits of red wine come from the tannins. Wines with higher tannins, like Cabernet Sauvignon, are more beneficial, in moderation.

300 | Cabernet Sauvignon is the offspring of grapevines grafted from Cabernet Franc and Sauvignon Blanc.

301 | *Phylloxera* are tiny insects that feed on the roots of vines. They nearly wiped out the wine industry when the bugs traveled on plants to France from America in the late 1850s. They have wreaked havoc here in America over the years as well.

302 | Rose bushes are sometimes planted in vineyards because they are often affected by diseases or mildew before the vines and act as predictors of trouble for grape growers.

303 | *Noble rot* is the beneficial form of botrytis, a fungus that aids in producing fine dessert wines.

304 | Wine-growing regions have felt more record-breaking temperatures in the last ten years than any preceding decade, an effect of climate change.

Wine History
and
Interesting Facts

305 | We say *cheers* in English, *salut* in Italian, *santé* in French, *prost* in German, and *sláinte* in Irish Gaelic!

306 | Marilyn Monroe once took a bath in Champagne using 350 bottles.

307 | *Sabrage* is the art of removing the top of the Champagne bottle with a saber for ceremonial occasions. It separates the collar from the bottle, exposing the Champagne for drinking.

308 | In the Bible, Noah planted a vineyard and fermented the grapes to make wine.

Memorable Wine Moments

It was a summer evening in Steamboat Springs, Colorado. My in-laws, whom I love dearly, were celebrating their anniversary. After dinner with a bottle of Caymus Cabernet Sauvignon, they brought out a special dessert wine that they brought back from France, where they lived when my husband was just a boy. We enjoyed the Château d'Yquem while listening to their stories of love and life in Bordeaux.

309 | The widow Clicquot was left a bankrupt business when her husband died. She took it over, basically creating the Champagne industry and becoming known as an infamous Champagne brand. Her picture is on the metal cork cover of Veuve Clicquot.

310 | *Oenophobia* is an intense hatred or fear of wine. *Oenophilia* is an intense love of wine. Now that's more like it!

311 | Dionysus was the Greek god of wine, and Bacchus was the roman god of wine, who created wine and viticulture. Ancient Greeks believed wine was a divine beverage.

312 | The word *Sauvignon* is believed to derive from the French word *sauvage*, which means wild.

313 | Pinot Noir was derived from the word *pin*, meaning pine, because the small grape clusters resembled a pinecone.

314 | A Starbucks tall latte has approximately the same number of calories as a glass of Champagne. I'll take the Champagne, please!

315 | The word *sommelier* is French and means wine steward, butler, or officer in charge of provisions. A sommelier during the French Revolution was responsible for tasting his lord's food to be sure it was not poisoned. The origin of the word is derived from the word *sauma*, meaning pack animal. There are four challenging levels of exams to become a certified Master Sommelier today through the Court of Master Sommeliers. The cool people call them *Somms*.

316 | Jeanne Calment, the world's oldest person whose age was well documented, was a 122-year-old lady from France who enjoyed a diet of olive oil, red wine, and chocolate!

317 | The tiny bubbles that travel up the side of your Champagne flute and form a ring is called a *collarette*.

318 | Champagne spraying has become a tradition with motorsports. It started in 1966 as an accident when a cork shot out of a bottle that had warmed in the sun and sprayed the crowd.

319 | The Champagne coupe is shorter and much wider than the Champagne flute. It is rumored to have been modeled after Marie Antoinette's breast. Personally, I love this classic glass style, but it is not as efficient at maintaining the bubbles.

320 | Pol Roger Champagne produced a special pint bottle for Winston Churchill that was served to him daily at lunchtime!

321 | Did you know you taste faster than you see, hear, or feel?

322 | The thicker and darker green wine bottle was invented in approximately 1650 by the English Sir Kenelm Digby.

323 | Stephen Spurrier was the British wine merchant who organized the 1976 blind Paris wine tasting that brought attention to California wines.

324 | Rosé was the first wine made in about 7,000 BCE. Red and white wine came thousands of years later.

325 | Red wine has more antioxidants than white wine, which can help prevent heart disease, raise HDL (good) cholesterol, lower LDL (bad) cholesterol, and prevent cancer cell growth.

326 | Red wine has melatonin, which comes from contact with the grape skins, that can help you sleep.

Memorable Wine Moments

I traveled to Vermont to attend a family wedding at the beautiful Mountain Top Inn. My mother is from there, and I spent much time there growing up. It isn't often that I have all four of my boys (Edward, Hayes, Jeffrey, and Alston) together, along with my sisters, my aunts, and my cousin, but I did that night. It was a feeling of fullness, completeness, and gratitude for me. We shared a bottle of River Angler Cabernet Sauvignon. We reconnected, laughed, danced, and celebrated family and love.

327 | Red and white wine residue was found in vessels left in the Egyptian Pharoah King Tut's tomb.

328 | In 2013, a hailstorm in France caused over €100 million worth of damage to vines—a year's worth of work destroyed in minutes.

329 | The best way to cultivate your sense of taste is to spend more time smelling, tasting, and identifying aromas. Drink up!

330 | Over 20 percent of the land in France is oak forest, some of which is used for oak barrels.

331 | Napa Valley contributes over $50 billion to the American economy annually.

332 | The average age of a French oak tree used to make wine barrels is 170 years.

333 | Cork is taken from the bark of the cork oak tree. The tree is not cut down, and the bark grows back. The cork can be harvested every nine years.

334 | Once cork is harvested, it needs to be dried. This can take up to two years.

335 | Wine drinkers have approximately a 34 percent lower mortality rate than drinkers of other alcohol.

336 | The first mention of a corkscrew was in the 1680s and was a steel worm on a musket barrel cleaning tool.

337 | The first corkscrew patent was in 1795. The wine key was patented in 1882, followed by the wing corkscrew patent in 1930. The biggest advance in the corkscrew occurred in 1979 with the invention of the Screwpull, with its advanced design and Teflon worm.

338 | The tariff on wine bottles from China went up here in the United States in 2019, initially 8 percent and then up 25 percent.

For the *Love of Wine*

339 | Red wine makes your blood vessels dilate, causing warm blood to move closer to the skin's surface, which can cause your face to flush.

340 | A case of wine weighs thirty to thirty-five pounds. France has moved to the six-bottle box because of its weight.

341 | The ancient Greeks preserved their wine by pouring olive oil on top of it to protect it from air.

Memorable Wine Moments

I brought my youngest two boys to see the Boston Pops Orchestra perform on the beach of Nantucket. I sipped The Daisies Sauvignon Blanc while we ate lobster rolls and played games on a blanket at the beach with the orchestra playing in the background. I loved sharing one of my favorite events with them, which culminated with the traditional playing of Tchaikovsky's 1812 Overture to fireworks. A spectacular event and memory.

342 The first book on wine was written in 1568 by William Turner. The first wine book I read was *Windows of the World Complete Wine Course* by Kevin Zraly. (It's great.) However, my favorite wine book of all time is *Reading Between the Wines* by Tery Theise. If you enjoy reading my book, you are going to love that one. I promise!

343 The word *booze* comes from the sixteenth century and was used to describe bad guys, thieves, and beggars.

344 The higher the alcohol content in wine, the higher the calories.

345 Historically, famous Bordeaux wines were offered as *futures* and purchased on speculation. In 2012, Château Latour stopped this practice, wanting to release it when it's ready directly to the consumer instead of using a middleman.

346 During prohibition, illegal saloons known as speakeasies arose. High-proof alcohol became popular as wineries diminished.

347 | After prohibition, sweet, cheap wines were popular until the mid-1960s when fine table wine emerged.

348 | Australia began using screw caps in 2000 with New Zealand following suit. Almost all wines from there now come in a screw-cap bottle.

349 | The *Titanic* holds the oldest-known wine cellar. Divers found most of the bottles intact.

350 | On Prince Charles's twenty-first birthday, Queen Elizabeth gave him an Aston Martin that runs on biofuel made out of wine.

351 | There is a spa in Japan where you can swim in wine.

352 | Romans started bumping wine glasses with a cheers, so wine would spill from one glass to another. This way they would be certain no one was poisoning the other.

353 | The term *toasting* originated when the Romans would drop a piece of toast into the wine prior to drinking it to make it taste better.

354 | Wine is cholesterol and fat-free!

355 | You pronounce the "t" in Moët & Chandon Champagne.

356 | China is the largest market for red wine—first because of flavor and second, believe it or not, because the color red is favored by the government and considered lucky.

357 | Wine consumption is predicted to continue growing over the next five years with Asia-Pacific seeing rapid growth.

358 | Madame de Pompadour, mistress of Louis XV, once hosted a ball where 1,800 bottles of Champagne were consumed. Some say this was the start of Champagne becoming a drink of celebration.

359 | Only approximately 10 percent of California wineries have female-led winemakers.

360 | The 2019–2020 fires in South Australia's wine district wiped out about one-third of their vines. It will take about seven years to achieve the regrowth.

361 | Piper-Heidsieck is the official Champagne of the Oscars. Corks are popped at the event about every eight seconds!

362 | Fewer people are collecting wine today, with millennials facing tough housing markets, student debt, and a more simplified lifestyle. Our wines are ready to enjoy today!

363 | A village in Northern Italy found wine flowing from their water taps in 2020! A valve malfunction at a nearby winery released hundreds of gallons of wine into the water system.

364
South America, Australia, New Zealand, and South Africa were in the midst of their harvest during the novel coronavirus COVID-19 lockdowns in 2020. Thankfully, the wineries were deemed essential!

365
Wine can enhance your meal, your conversation, and your connections with family and friends!

Memorable Wine Moments

My husband, Scott, and I drove to Denver in a rented truck to pick up several hundreds of gallons of wine shipped from California. It was an unusually hot September day. While driving home through the mountains, our truck began to overheat. We were on the side of a major highway with no breakdown lane and no cellphone reception. The drums were too heavy for us to move, and if they sat there for hours, the wine would spoil. We lifted the hood to see if it would cool down, but it was over 90 degrees outside. I feared I would lose tens of thousands of dollars, and I said out loud, "I am calling on our angels, Jane and Jeff (my mother and Scott's late brother), to carry us on their wings." Within minutes, a rare hailstorm erupted, snow covered us and the road, everything cooled, and we were able to drive home. We shared a bottle of The Antlers Reserve Cabernet Sauvignon at home that evening and toasted to our angels.

About the Author

Penney Adams has had a lifelong affinity for wine. Her father was a wine collector of fine French Bordeaux and Napa Cabernet Sauvignon. Her family had wine on the dinner table as long as she can remember. She has an undergraduate degree in English and a master's degree in business from Queens University. She is currently studying for the second-level exam with the Court of Master Sommeliers. She previously owned a retail wine store, The Wine Gallery, that featured fine wine and art. She currently lives in Steamboat Springs, Colorado, with her husband and two of her four boys. She established Steamboat Winery, LLC in 2017. Purchasing grapes from California gives her the ability to produce an exquisite wine in the skiing, fishing, and ranching community of Steamboat Springs. Her hope is that you will enjoy this book, as well as her wines, with family and friends, enhancing your meal and cultivating great conversation, connection, laughter, love, and memories you will savor for a lifetime.

Bibliography

Parker, Robert, "The Wine Advocate Vintage Guide." Robert Parker Wine Advocate, 2019.
https://www.robertparker.com/resources/vintage-chart

Pomranz, Mike, "These States Drink the Most Wine Per Capita." Food & Wine, 01/08/19.
https://www.foodandwine.com/news/wine-drinking-state-national-institutes-health

Thatch, Liz, "The US Wine Industry in 2020 - Slowing Sales, but Opportunities Still Present (with COVID-19 Update)." Dr. Liz Thatch, MW, 2/24/20.
https://lizthachmw.com/2020/02/24/the-us-wine-industry-in-2020-slowing-sales-but-opportunities-still-present/

Quinlan, Christine, "8 Health Benefits of Drinking Wine." Food & Wine, 06/14/17.
https://www.foodandwine.com/wine/red-wine/8-health-benefits-of-drinking-wine

Willcox, Kathleen, "How Millenials Are Changing the Wine-Selling Game." Regal Wine, 9/20/2017.
https://www.regalwine.com/2017/10/millennials-changing-wine-selling-game/

Savor the Wine.
Savor the Moments.
Savor the Memories.

Learn more about the wines in this book and create your own memorable wine moments by visiting
steamboatwinery.com

or follow us on social media.

 @Steamboat Winery   @steamboatwinery